FOOD IN FOCUS

Bread

Jenny Ridgwell

First published in Great Britain by Heinemann Library
Halley Court, Jordan Hill, Oxford OX2 8EJ,
a division of Reed Educational and Professional Publishing Ltd.

Heinemann is a registered trademark of Reed Educational and
Professional Publishing Ltd.

OXFORD FLORENCE PRAGUE MADRID ATHENS
MELBOURNE AUCKLAND KUALA LUMPUR SINGAPORE TOKYO
IBADAN NAIROBI KAMPALA JOHANNESBURG GABORONE
PORTSMOUTH NH (USA) CHICAGO MEXICO CITY SAO PAULO

Designed by Celia Floyd
Illustrations by Barry Atkinson, pp. 9, 10, 12, 13, 20, 23, 24, 26, 28;
Oxford Illustrators, pp. 8, 17
Printed in Hong Kong / China

02 01 00 99 98
10 9 8 7 6 5 4 3 2 1

ISBN 0 431 08872 1

British Library Cataloguing in Publication Data

Ridgwell, Jenny
    Bread. - (Food in focus)
    1.Bread - Juvenile literature
    I.Title
    664.7'523

Acknowledgements

The Publishers would like to thank the following for permission to reproduce
photographs:

APV Baker, p. 7; Bridgeman Art Library, p. 6; Gareth Boden, pp. 4, 11, 14, 18, 21, 25,
27, 29; Robert Harding Picture Library, p. 5 (Robert Frerck); SIS Marketing, p. 19; Trip,
p. 15, Ask Images, p. 15 (bottom), H. Rogers

Cover photograph: Trevor Clifford

Every effort has been made to contact copyright holders of any material reproduced in
this book. Any omissions will be rectified in subsequent printings if notice is given to
the Publisher.

Contents

● ● ● ● ● ● ● ● ● ● ● ● ● ● ● ● ● ● ●

Some words are shown in bold, **like this**. You can find out what they mean by looking in the Glossary.

Introduction

What can bread be used for?

Bread is one of the most important foods that is eaten around the world. It is a valuable food for health. It gives us energy, vitamins, minerals and fibre which help to keep our digestive system healthy.

Bread comes in many shapes and sizes. It is made into loaves, bagels, baps, muffins, buns and rolls. Bread is too precious to be wasted and there are famous recipes made from leftover bread, such as bread and butter pudding.

Around the world bread comes in many shapes and sizes

What is it like?

The basic ingredients for breadmaking are flour and water. Wheat flour is the most popular as it contains **gluten** which is the protein that forms the structure and shape of the bread when it is baked or cooked by other methods. Flat breads, such as crispbreads, are made without **raising agents**. These are the substances which are added to baking mixtures, such as bread or cake mixtures, to make them rise. Flat breads are called **unleavened breads**. **Leavened breads** are lighter than unleavened breads as they are made using raising agents which help the bread to rise. The dough is pushed up by a raising agent, such as **yeast** or baking powder.

Other ingredients give flavour and colour to bread recipes. Eggs, butter, sugar, spices and dried fruits, like sultanas and cherries, are used to make delicious sweet breads. Savoury breads can be made from many ingredients including cheese, olives, dried tomatoes and herbs.

Bread is cooked in different ways. Most breads are baked in an oven, but bread can be cooked on metal plates or griddles and in a tandoor, a clay oven which can be heated with hot charcoal.

Why and when do we eat it?

In many countries, bread is eaten with meals and it is also a popular snack food eaten throughout the day. Bread can be eaten on its own, it can be spread with butter and other toppings, such as jam, marmalade and peanut butter, or it can be made into toast. In European countries, such as France and Italy, crusty bread is eaten with meals. In Asia and South America, breads like chapatis and tortillas are used to dip into stews and soups. In the Middle East, flat pitta breads are split open and stuffed with salad and meat.

Millions of sandwiches made from bread are eaten at lunchtime and are often sold ready-made from sandwich bars and supermarkets.

These people in Mexico are eating tortillas as a quick snack

History of breadmaking

Bread is one of the oldest foods in the world and was discovered over 5000 years ago. Early breads were made from grass seeds ground into flour, mixed with water and baked on a hot stone. The Ancient Egyptians were the first people to grind wheat and make it into bread. They were nicknamed the 'bread eaters' because they ate so much bread. At the time, bread was used instead of money and the workers who built the pyramids were paid in bread.

Flat, **unleavened bread** is made from flour and water and contains no **raising agent**. However, if you leave a mixture of flour and water for a few days it becomes bubbly. This is because **yeasts** in the air mix with the dough and react with it. This produces bubbles of **carbon dioxide** gas. This type of 'wild yeast' dough is known as **sourdough**. Today we add yeast to many bread recipes to make the bread rise.

A model of Egyptian servants making bread from around 2000 BC

Brown or white bread?

Through the ages most people ate coarse, wholemeal bread because white flour was expensive to make. In the nineteenth century, the way wheat was ground into flour was improved by machinery. White flour became cheaper and many more people could afford to eat white bread. Today, white bread is more popular than wholemeal bread but experts recommend that we eat more bread of every kind, particularly wholemeal bread which is rich in nutrients and fibre.

For centuries bread has been cooked in the home in ovens or on griddles. Small bakeries started in Roman times to bake bread for customers in villages and towns. In many countries around the world, people still buy their bread every day fresh from the local bakery. Most of our bread is now made in factory bakeries and sold in large supermarkets, that may also have in-store bakeries making a range of freshly baked breads throughout the day.

Modern bakeries produce thousands of loaves of bread a day

Did you know?

- *The person who earns money for the family is often called the breadwinner.*
- *The Great Fire of London in 1666 was started by a baker and destroyed the baking industry in the city.*

Growing ingredients for bread

Flour for breadmaking can be made from grains of cereals, such as wheat, barley, oats, maize and rye, or from dried roots, such as potato and cassava.

When a cereal grain or root grows well in an area, it becomes a **staple food** for the people who live there. A staple food, such as bread, forms a large part of the diet.

Cereal grains

Wheat is the best cereal grain for breadmaking. It grows in temperate, cool areas of the world, in countries including USA, Canada, Russia and Australia. Today wheat bread is eaten in many countries around the world.

Maize or Indian corn originated from the Americas and was taken to Europe by Christopher Columbus and other explorers. The crop became popular in Asia and Africa. Maize grows well in sunny climates including USA, and is made into breads and breakfast cereals.

Rye is an important cereal grain in northern Europe and grows well in cool climates in poor soil. Rye breads are popular in Germany and Russia.

Oats grow in cool climates such as northern Europe. Traditional oatcakes come from Scotland.

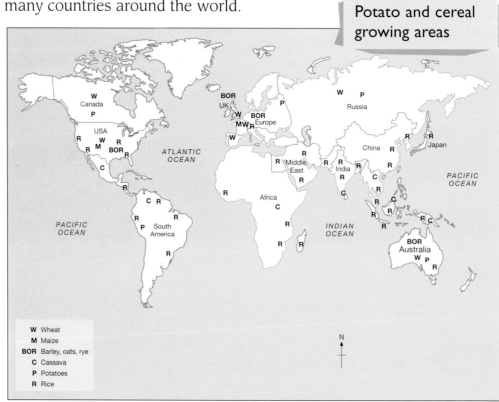

Potato and cereal growing areas

W Wheat
M Maize
BOR Barley, oats, rye
C Cassava
P Potatoes
R Rice

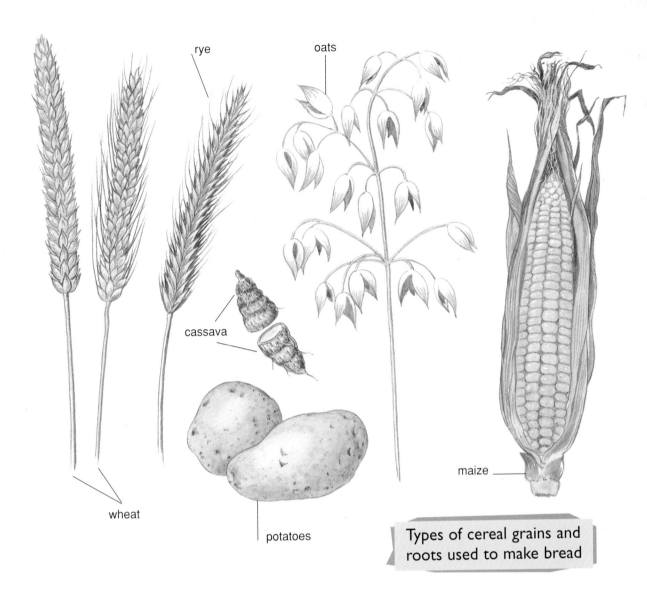

rye

oats

cassava

maize

wheat

potatoes

Types of cereal grains and roots used to make bread

Root crops

Potatoes came from South America. Today this important food crop is grown in most parts of the world. Potato flour can be used for breadmaking but potatoes are usually eaten as vegetables.

Cassava is a root which comes from South America and is an important food plant in the tropics. The roots are grated and made into a powder called meal which can then be used for making bread.

People in rice-growing areas, such as parts of China, India and Indonesia, eat boiled rice as their staple food instead of bread. As food is exported around the world, traditional rice-eating countries are eating more bread, and rice is a popular part of the diet in countries that previously had bread as their staple food.

How is bread made?

Bread is usually made from wheat flour, water and salt. **Unleavened bread** is flat and contains no **raising agents** to make it rise. **Leavened bread** uses a raising agent, such as **yeast** to make the bread rise. Bread can be made in many different ways depending upon the type of recipe.

Making leavened bread

What to do:

1 Flour, salt and warm water are mixed together with the yeast to make a soft dough.
2 The dough is **kneaded** to make it smooth and elastic and to stretch the **gluten** in the flour.
3 The dough is shaped into a loaf and left in a warm place to **prove** and increase in size.
4 The loaf is baked in a hot oven. Bubbles of gas are produced when yeast **ferments** and these bubbles help the bread to rise. The bubbles of gas expand in the heat and push up the bread dough. The dough sets and cooks until the outside is crisp and firm.

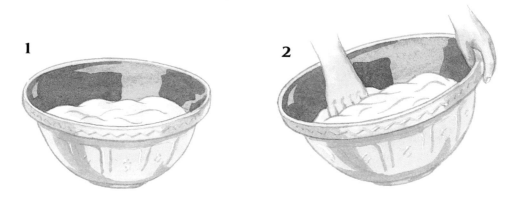

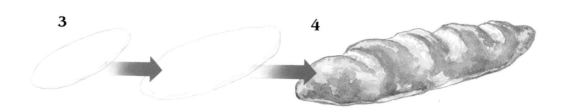

The ingredients

Yeast

Most bread recipes use fresh or dried yeast. Yeast is a single-celled plant fungus which is used to make bread rise. Yeast needs food (from the flour), liquid (the water) and warmth in order to grow, ferment and produce bubbles of gas which help the bread to rise.

Flour

Flour for breadmaking can be made from cereal grains, such as wheat, barley, oats, maize and rye, or from dried roots, such as potato and cassava.

Strong wheat flour is best for breadmaking as it contains the most gluten. Gluten is a protein in flour and it helps to form the shape and framework of the bread. When bread dough is kneaded, the gluten is stretched and this improves the quality, texture and structure of the baked bread.

Liquid

Water or a liquid, like milk, is used to mix the ingredients together. The liquid should be warm to speed up the breadmaking process. However, if the liquid is too hot, the yeast will be killed and the bread will not rise.

Salt

Salt is an essential ingredient in bread. It provides flavour and helps to give bread a good shape and texture.

Lots of other ingredients can be added to bread to give flavour and texture. Delicious savoury breads are made with crunchy seeds, nuts, cheese, herbs and vegetables, such as dried tomatoes. Dried fruits, spices and sugar are mixed with the bread dough to make sweet breads, such as teacakes and hot cross buns.

Bread is made from flour, liquid, yeast and salt

Flours for breadmaking

Wheat flours

Wheat is the most popular cereal grain used for breadmaking. Wheat flour is made by **milling** or grinding clean grains of wheat.

The wheat grain is made up of three important parts:

- endosperm makes up 85% of the grain and is used to make white flour
- bran makes up 12% of the grain. It is the outside husk and provides dietary fibre
- wheatgerm makes up 3% of the grain and contains vitamins and minerals.

Different sorts of flour use different proportions of the parts of the wheat grain.

White flour is made from the endosperm.

Brown flour is a mixture of white flour and bran.

Wheatgerm flour is white or brown flour with added wheatgerm.

Wholemeal flour is made from all parts of the wheat grain.

Stoneground flour is wholemeal flour ground in a traditional way between two stones.

A strong flour is best for breadmaking as the high protein content makes bread with a good structure and open texture. Strong flour comes from wheat which has grown in lots of sun, so that the wheat grain develops plenty of protein.

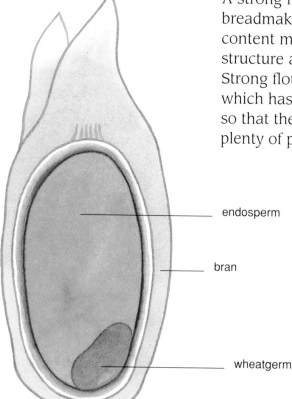

endosperm

bran

wheatgerm

The inside of a wheat grain

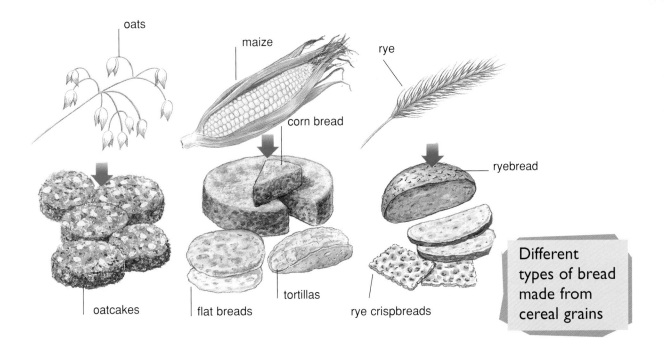

oats

maize

rye

corn bread

ryebread

oatcakes

flat breads

tortillas

rye crispbreads

Different types of bread made from cereal grains

Other flours

Other cereal grains and roots which can be made into bread include oats, maize, rye, barley, potato and cassava. Each flour gives a special flavour, texture and colour to the bread.

Oats are ground into oatmeal and made into flat oatcakes. Oatcakes are made from oatmeal, water, salt and fat which are mixed into a dough and pressed into thin biscuits and cooked in an oven. They are popular in Scotland. To make a lightly risen bread, oatmeal needs to be mixed with wheat flour.

Maize or corn is ground into cornmeal and made into a soft, yellow cornbread which is popular in the southern United States. In Mexico, maize flour is made into flat pancake-like tortillas.

Rye produces a darker flour than wheat. The flour is made into rye crispbreads and bread which is dark brown and firm to the touch. This bread is popular in northern Europe and Scandinavia.

Barley flour makes bread and baked products such as scones.

Potato flour is a fine white powder which can be used alone or mixed with wheat flour for bread.

Cassava flour is made from the tropical starchy root. The root is grated, dried and made into bread, cakes and wafers.

Some people like to eat **organic food** which is produced without the use of pesticides and fertilizers. Organic flour is milled from wheat which is grown and processed naturally without the use of chemicals. Organic foods are often more expensive since the crops produce lower yields.

Bread around the world

There are thousands of varieties of breads from around the world.

Flat breads include crispbreads from Scandinavia and Mexican tortillas. Tortillas are grilled on large, flat iron pans and eaten with spicy stews and snacks. In India, Pakistan and Bangladesh flat breads are served at mealtimes.

Chapatis are made by rolling the dough into a disc shape and cooking it on a metal plate called a tawa.

Parathas are heavier, layered breads, sometimes filled with vegetables.

Flat breads include pitta and tortillas

Naan bread is usually made with **yeast** and cooked in a tandoor.

Matza is an **unleavened bread** which is made without **raising agents** (the substances which are added to a baking mixture, such as a bread mixture, to make it rise). This bread is eaten by Jewish people at Passover. It represents the departure of the Israelites from Egypt when there was no time to let the bread rise.

Bread can be shaped by cooking it in special tins to make loaves for slicing. It can also be moulded into shapes, such as cottage loaves and French sticks, or the dough can be twisted, plaited and decorated by cutting it with a cross or slashes.

Irish soda bread is made using baking soda instead of yeast as a raising agent. Pumpernickel and rye bread are popular breads in northern Europe and are made from rye flour.

Hard dough bread comes from the Caribbean. The dough has sugar added to it and is made using a long **proving** process so that the bread is firm and sweet.

Special occasions

Breads are made for special occasions such as festivals and feasts. Hot cross buns are small fruit buns with a cross on top and are eaten at Easter time. Greek Easter bread has coloured, hard boiled eggs baked in the bread.

In Mexico, bread is made for the *Dia de Muertos* (the Day of the Dead) on November 2nd.

Challah bread is usually eaten on the Jewish Sabbath. This bread is plaited and can be broken into pieces for serving.

Panettone is a Christmas bread from northern Italy which is made with candied fruit and raisins.

Harvest bread is made in Britain to celebrate the harvest in the autumn which is when the ripe cereal grains are gathered. Harvest bread is shaped like a traditional wheat sheaf which is the old way of stacking the wheat for it to dry in the fields.

Special bread is made for the Mexican Day of the Dead

Harvest bread is made in the shape of a wheat sheaf

How is sliced bread made?

Large 'plant' bakeries make most of the bread that we eat. These bakeries often work twenty-four hours a day, seven days a week to produce billions of perfectly baked loaves of bread.

The ingredients

The basic ingredients for bread baked on a large scale are flour, salt, **improver** (which speeds up the breadmaking process), **yeast** and water. Many types of flour can be used for the bread. These include white, wholemeal and brown flours. Extra ingredients such as oats, granary flakes and wheatgerm can be added according to the recipe chosen.

Computer control

Bread baking in large bakeries is controlled by a vast computer system. The ingredients are precisely measured and the computer controls the baking process to make sure the loaves have the same texture, taste and weight every time.

Large bakeries can produce billions of perfectly baked loaves every week

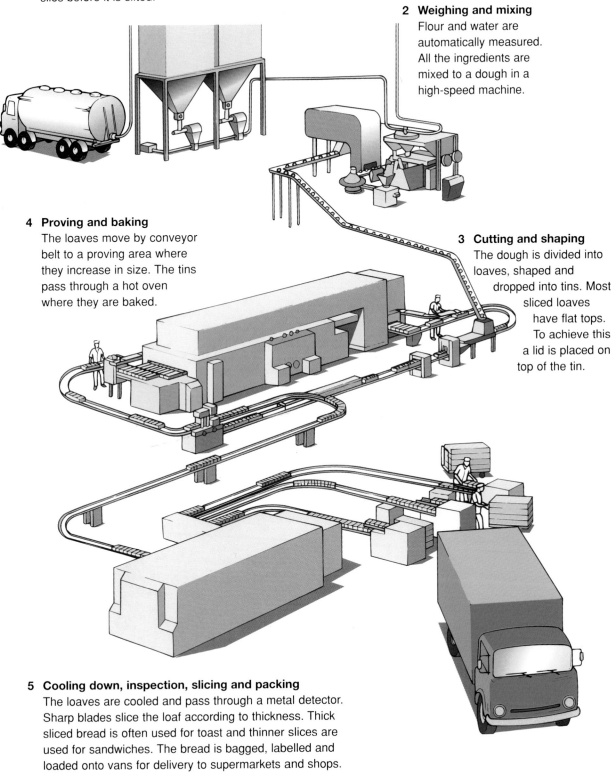

1 Delivery and storage
Flour arrives at the bakeries in tankers and is stored in silos before it is sifted.

2 Weighing and mixing
Flour and water are automatically measured. All the ingredients are mixed to a dough in a high-speed machine.

4 Proving and baking
The loaves move by conveyor belt to a proving area where they increase in size. The tins pass through a hot oven where they are baked.

3 Cutting and shaping
The dough is divided into loaves, shaped and dropped into tins. Most sliced loaves have flat tops. To achieve this a lid is placed on top of the tin.

5 Cooling down, inspection, slicing and packing
The loaves are cooled and pass through a metal detector. Sharp blades slice the loaf according to thickness. Thick sliced bread is often used for toast and thinner slices are used for sandwiches. The bread is bagged, labelled and loaded onto vans for delivery to supermarkets and shops.

Bread today

Ways of buying and packing bread

In recent years, bread products and packaging have been designed to save time and to help bread keep for longer.

Gas packing extends the shelf life of packaged bread. The shelf life is the amount of time the product can be kept and still be safe and good to eat. The air inside the packaging is replaced with a mixture of **carbon dioxide** and nitrogen gas which delays the growth of moulds which may grow in bread. Gas packing is used for bagels, bread, part-baked breads and pitta bread.

Additives in bread

The additives that are used in food are strictly tested. Your choice of foods would be reduced if additives were not used. The additives in wrapped bread are shown on the label. These may include vitamin C (ascorbic acid) which improves the texture of the bread, and emulsifying agents and preservatives to help the bread stay fresh for a longer time and so improve the shelf life of the product.

Bread products can be packed with special gas packing to help them stay fresh longer

Bread changes for diet and health

Some people have a condition known as coeliac disease and are allergic to **gluten**. Gluten is the protein found in wheat and other flours which helps to form the bread framework. People who are allergic to gluten can buy or make bread made from gluten-free flours which come from a variety of cereal grains, such as maize and rice, which do not contain gluten.

We are encouraged to eat more fibre but many people like to eat white bread. A new softgrain white bread has been produced with fibre which comes from peas and beans to give a fibre-rich choice.

If you like the taste of freshly baked bread, you can buy part-baked bread which has been partly cooked and finish the cooking yourself. If you like homemade bread, a breadmaking machine is simple to use. Put all the ingredients into the machine and set the dials. The machine mixes, **kneads**, **proves** and cooks the dough in the one container. Kneading is the process of pulling and stretching the dough to improve the texture of the baked bread. Proving is the step in the breadmaking process when the bread dough is left in a warm place to increase in size. When the loaf is baked take it out of the machine, cool it and it is ready to eat.

An electric bread machine

Bread and health

The healthy diet pyramid

Bread is an important food in a healthy diet. The **healthy diet pyramid** shows how to make healthy food choices. Our diet should contain a wide variety of different foods in order to provide the range of nutrients that we need.

The healthy diet pyramid suggests that we eat plenty of bread, cereal grains, rice and pasta and lots of fruit and vegetables. These foods are shown in the lower section of the pyramid.

Foods from the top of the pyramid include fats, oils and sugary foods. For better health we should eat less of these foods.

How healthy is bread?

Bread is a nutritious food. It provides us with energy, fibre, vitamins and minerals which we need for our daily lives.

Over 50% of our energy intake should come from fibre-rich carbohydrate foods like bread. Nutrition experts suggest that we eat up to six slices of bread a day.

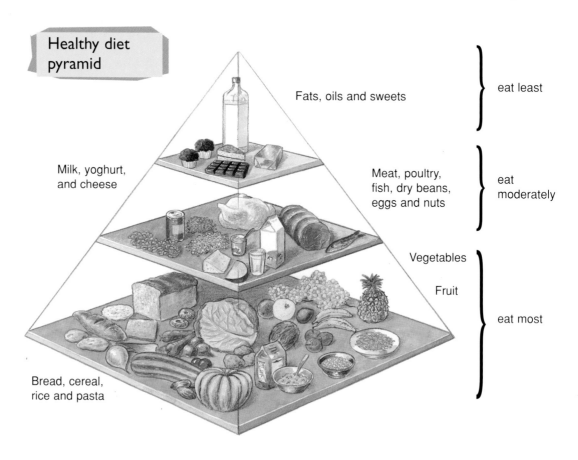

Healthy diet pyramid

Fats, oils and sweets — eat least

Milk, yoghurt, and cheese

Meat, poultry, fish, dry beans, eggs and nuts — eat moderately

Vegetables

Fruit

eat most

Bread, cereal, rice and pasta

Complex carbohydrates

Bread is a major source of carbohydrate in the form of starch, a **complex carbohydrate**. This is a long-lasting energy source so bread is filling without providing too many **calories**.

Energy

The energy from bread, in the form of calories, comes mostly from carbohydrate. Bread is a low fat food and is not fattening. It is the fat that you add, such as butter and spreads, that increases the calories.

We should eat six slices of bread a day as part of a healthy diet

Fibre

Cereal grain products, including all types of bread, are good sources of fibre. Fibre is important to prevent constipation. Wholemeal and brown bread have more fibre than white bread.

Protein

Bread provides protein which is needed for growth, maintenance and repair of the body.

Calcium and iron

Calcium is a mineral needed for strong bones and teeth. Iron is needed for healthy blood. Bread provides calcium and iron and in the UK white flour is fortified with these minerals.

B vitamins

Cereal grain products such as bread are good sources of the B vitamins which are needed for good health.

Experiments with yeast

Raising agents are added to mixtures, such as bread and cakes, to make them rise. **Yeast** is a raising agent which is often used in breadmaking. Yeast is a single-celled plant fungus. The cells are so small that they can only be seen under a microscope. Always wash your hands before and after handling yeast.

Yeast under the microscope

You will need:

- fresh and dried yeast
- water
- 2 microscope slides
- a microscope

What to do:

1 Take some fresh yeast and mix it with a little water.
2 Smear some of this mixture onto a microscope slide.
3 Place the slide under the microscope and focus the lens so that you can see the yeast cells.
4 Repeat the experiment using dried yeast.
5 Compare the shape and size of the fresh and dried yeast cells as seen under the microscope.

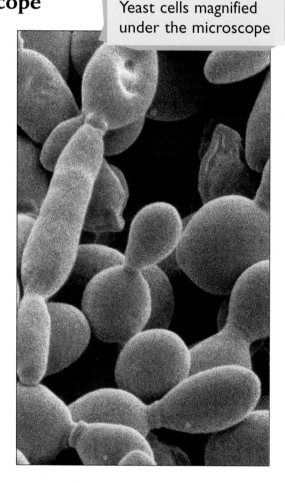

Yeast cells magnified under the microscope

When bread is made, the yeast grows and **ferments** and gives off **carbon dioxide** gas and alcohol. This carbon dioxide gas expands during breadmaking and baking and pushes up the dough.

What does yeast need to grow and ferment?

You will need:

- fresh or dried yeast
- 5 ml spoon (teaspoon)
- sugar
- 4 small glass bottles
- water
- 4 balloons to cover each bottle
- digital scales
- 4 labels
- 15 ml spoon (tablespoon)
- washing up bowl

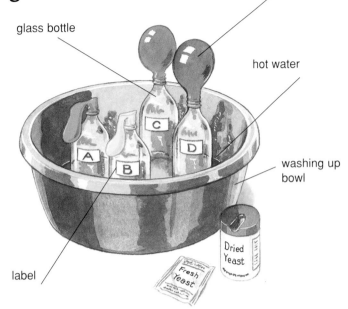

What to do:

Label the bottles A, B, C and D.
Put 2.5 g ($\frac{1}{2}$ teaspoon) yeast (fresh or dried) into each.

3 Add one 15 ml spoonful cold water to A.
   Add one 15 ml spoonful warm water to B.
   Add one 15 ml spoonful cold water and one 5 ml spoonful sugar to C.
   Add one 15 ml spoonful warm water and one 5 ml spoonful sugar to D.

4 Put your finger over the end of each bottle and shake thoroughly. Cover the end of each with a balloon.

5 Stand all the bottles in a bowl of hot water for 20 minutes.

6 Watch what happens to each of the yeast mixtures and the balloons. Do any of the balloons blow up? Which ones?

What should happen?

Yeast needs food (the sugar), liquid (the water) and warmth to grow and ferment. In experiment D, the yeast feeds on the sugar and grows in the warm water to produce carbon dioxide gas. When this gas is produced, the balloon blows up. You may find the balloon on C blows up because the mixture becomes warm from the water in the washing up bowl. The balloons in experiments A and B will not blow up because the yeast has no food so it cannot grow and produce carbon dioxide gas.

Try changing this experiment. Try adding salt or flour instead of sugar or see what happens if you use boiling water.

Wholemeal bread rolls

• •

This bread roll recipe is based upon a traditional European recipe which uses fresh **yeast**. To speed things up easyblend yeast has been used in this case. You can make these bread rolls into a variety of shapes – round rolls, small cottage loaves, plaits and twists. To make a loaf from this recipe put all of the mixture into a bread tin and allow extra cooking time. Before you start ask an adult to help.

You will need:

Makes 8 rolls

Ingredients

- 500 g strong wholemeal bread flour
- 1 teaspoon (5 ml) salt
- 1 x 7 g sachet easyblend yeast
- 1 tablespoon vegetable oil
- 300 ml lukewarm water
- extra flour for kneading
- extra oil for brushing
- toppings – flaked oats, flour, sesame seeds or poppy seeds

Equipment

- scales
- pastry brush
- large mixing bowl
- teaspoon, tablespoon, wooden spoon
- measuring jug
- baking sheet
- cling film
- oven gloves
- wire rack

What to do:

1 Set the oven at Gas Mark 8, 230°C. Brush the baking sheet with a little oil to prevent the bread rolls from sticking during baking.
2 Mix together the flour, salt and easyblend yeast in a bowl.
3 Using a wooden spoon gradually stir in the oil and lukewarm water until the mixture forms a soft but not sticky dough. You may not need to add all the water.
4 Turn the dough out onto a floured surface. Knead the dough by pushing and stretching it with your hands for 8–10 minutes.
5 Put the dough on a floured surface and roll into a sausage shape. Divide the dough into 8 equally sized pieces.
6 Roll each piece of dough into a smooth ball and place on a baking sheet.
7 Cover the bread rolls with cling film which has been brushed with oil.
8 Leave in a warm place to prove until the rolls have doubled in size.
9 Remove the cling film and sprinkle some flaked oats, flour, sesame or poppy seeds on the top of each roll.
10 Bake near the top of the oven until the rolls are golden brown (approx. 15 minutes). Take out of the oven using oven gloves and cool on a wire rack.

These wholemeal bread rolls were dusted with flour before cooking

Soda bread with cheese and herbs

• •

This recipe is like a traditional Irish soda bread, with added cheese and herbs. You can eat soda bread with soup and salads or sliced for sandwiches. Bicarbonate of soda is used as the **raising agent** instead of **yeast**. You can change the flavour of the bread by adding other ingredients, such as dried fruit, glacé cherries and sugar. Before you start ask an adult to help.

You will need:

Makes 1 loaf to serve 4 people.

Ingredients

- 200 g wholemeal bread flour
- 50 g plain white flour
- 20 g rolled oats
- 1 teaspoon (5 ml) bicarbonate of soda
- 1 teaspoon (5 ml) salt
- 50 g grated cheese
- $\frac{1}{2}$ teaspoon mixed dried herbs
- 170–200 ml milk
- extra flour for kneading
- cooking oil

Equipment

- scales
- pastry brush
- large mixing bowl
- teaspoon
- wooden spoon
- measuring jug
- baking sheet
- knife
- oven gloves
- wire rack

What to do:

1 Set the oven at Gas Mark 6, 200°C. Brush the baking sheet with a little oil to prevent the bread from sticking during baking.

2 Mix together the flours, oats, bicarbonate of soda, salt, cheese and herbs in a bowl.

3 Gradually stir in enough milk to make a stiff dough.

4 Turn the dough out onto a floured surface. Knead the dough for 2 minutes.

5 Shape into a large round loaf and place on the oiled baking sheet. Cut a deep cross in the top using a knife.

6 Bake in a hot oven for 30 minutes until the bottom of the loaf sounds hollow when tapped.

7 Take out of the oven using oven gloves and cool on a wire rack.

Soda bread

Fruity pizza

Pizzas were originally an ancient Roman breakfast food made from bread baked with cheese. Today pizzas are eaten in many parts of the world. They are made with a huge range of savoury and sweet toppings. For this fruit pizza you can use fresh or canned pieces of fruit for the topping. Pizzas can be eaten as a snack or this fruity pizza may be served as a dessert. Before you start ask an adult to help.

You will need:

Makes 2 pizzas to serve 4 people

Ingredients

- 225 g strong bread flour
- 1 teaspoon (5 ml) salt
- 1 x 7 g sachet easyblend yeast
- $\frac{1}{2}$ level teaspoon allspice or cinnamon
- 15 g granulated sugar
- about 150 ml lukewarm milk
- extra flour for kneading
- cooking oil

Topping:
- 100 g soft white cheese such as Mascarpone
- 2 tablespoons runny honey
- fruit topping: slices of fruit such as banana, pineapple, mandarin orange, cherries

Equipment

- scales
- pastry brush
- large mixing bowl
- small mixing bowl
- teaspoon, tablespoon, wooden spoon
- measuring jug
- rolling pin
- baking sheet
- oven gloves
- knife
- chopping board

What to do:

1 Set the oven at Gas Mark 8, 230°C. Brush the baking sheet with a little oil to prevent the pizzas from sticking during baking.

2 Mix together the flour, salt, easyblend yeast, allspice and sugar in a bowl.

3 Using a wooden spoon gradually stir in the lukewarm milk until the mixture forms a soft but not sticky dough. You may need to add more milk, depending upon the dryness of the mixture.

4 Turn the dough out onto a floured surface. Knead the dough by pushing and stretching it with your hands for 8–10 minutes.

5 Roll the dough on a floured surface into two circles about 16–20 cm in diameter using a rolling pin. Place on the baking sheet.

6 Mix together the soft cheese and one tablespoon of honey. Spread this mixture on the 2 pizza bases.

7 Slice up the fruit and place on the top of the pizzas. Spoon the remaining honey over the fruit.

8 Leave the pizzas in a warm place to prove until they have doubled in size.

9 Bake near the top of the oven for about 15 minutes until the pizzas are firm underneath.

10 Take out of the oven using oven gloves.

11 Eat warm or cold with some more fresh fruit or ice-cream.

Fruity pizza

Glossary

calorie a unit used to measure the energy value of food

carbon dioxide the gas produced when yeast ferments which helps the bread to rise by creating bubbles of gas

complex carbohydrate a carbohydrate in the form of starch

ferment to cause the chemical change which takes place during bread making and helps the bread to rise. The process is known as fermentation

gas packing changing the air in the package so that the food will keep longer

gluten a protein in flour which helps to form the bread framework, which is the structure or shape of the loaf or roll

healthy diet pyramid a system designed to show how to make healthy food choices

improver a substance added to the bread dough during large scale manufacture to speed up the breadmaking process

kneading stretching the dough to improve the quality and texture of the baked bread

leavened bread bread made using a raising agent such as yeast or baking soda which helps the bread to rise

milling the process of grinding the cereal grain into flour

organic food food produced without the use of pesticides and fertilizers

prove when bread dough is left in a warm place to allow the dough to increase in size

raising agent a substance added to a baking mixture, such as a bread or cake mixture to help it to rise

sourdough a dough which can be made from wild yeast

staple food a food, such as bread, which forms a large part of the diet

unleavened bread flat bread which does not use a raising agent such as yeast. Unleavened breads include chapatis

yeast a single-celled plant fungus which is used to make bread rise

Further reading

Developing Skills in Home Economics. C. Connell, D. Nutter, P. Tickner, J. Ridgwell. Heinemann Educational Australia, 1991

Food Around the World. Jenny Ridgwell and Judy Ridgway. Oxford University Press, 1986

Healthy Eating, Recipes and Investigations. Jenny Ridgwell and Judy Ridgway. Oxford University Press, 1989

Skills in Home Economics: Food. Jenny Ridgwell. Heinemann Educational, 1990

Useful addresses

Australian Nutrition Foundation, 1–3 Derwent Street, Glebe, NSW, Australia 2037

Federation of Bakers, 20 Bedford Square, London WC1B 3HF, UK

Flour Advisory Bureau, 21 Arlington Street, London SW1A 1RN, UK

The New Food Label, US Food and Drug Administration, International

Index